Nicki has been involved in the spiritual and paranormal world all her life. This has enabled her to gain great insight and knowledge on her journey thus far. She lives in Worcestershire with her husband and along with her writing Nicki also works as a Spiritual Life Coach.

To all that have helped me on my journey thus far...be
they in spirit or in person.

For the
Healing Angels.
with love.

Nicki Leonie

SOUL REFLECTIONS

AUST N MACAULEY
PUBLISHERS LTD.

A CIP catalogue record for this title is available from the British Library.

ISBN 978 184963 693 3

www.austinmacauley.com

First Published (2014)
Austin Macauley Publishers Ltd
25 Canada Square
Canary Wharf
London
E14 5LB

Printed and bound in Great Britain

Acknowledgments

Thank you to Austin Macauley Publishers for their hard work in bringing this book to fruition.

1
YOUR SOUL

Each Soul is formed from pure energy

The energy that surrounds us

That is part of us all

That forms all that exists

That is the Web of Life

Our Soul allows us to be

It is the reason we exist

It is all that we are

And all that we hope to be

An old Soul already holds knowledge

Though it is kept deep within

We can feel this knowledge if we choose

Each life adds more knowledge

Each new lesson allows us to learn more

Our knowledge knows no limits

Our learning is endless

Our ability to learn varies

Each soul keeps different knowledge

A new Soul holds a blank canvas

On to which life will paint many pictures

Each picture holds many colours

Each colour will influence our lives

The colours help to guide us

We use colour to bring balance

Harmony comes from colour

Colour surrounds us in life

We absorb colour

If negative we should change to positive

During our lives our Soul grows

This gives us depth

It learns empathy and humility

Without these qualities we do not truly learn

Those absorbed in themselves can never give

Therefore they will never receive

Those who expect to achieve will not

They will fail at each task

To receive you must first give

This must be unconditional

Only then do we receive rewards

Our Soul understands where we have been

Where we are now

And where we are going

Even though we may not

An understanding of ourselves we crave

We need a reason to be

But we do not understand the questions

Within all of us there are these answers

To go within the hardest of tasks

But brings us the greatest of knowledge

We need to take time to listen to our Soul

Deafness brings confusion within our lives

Many lives are spent in this confusion

This stops our progress and growth

Preventing Soul nourishment within

We spend time searching outside

This is to find our inner peace

Not realising answers are much closer

To reach inside needs honesty

The journey to self our hardest

Old Souls hold the greater wisdom

Their path is hardest to follow

Their confusion often the greatest

Their need to listen strongest

Their tasks in life the hardest

They are here to help others

Turbulent are their lives, taxing to extreme

These are the Souls who most aid others

They bring about change

We must cherish our Soul

It is who we are

It feels as we feel

It teaches us to be

It is us collectively and singularly

We are of energy

We are affected by energy

We feel changes in this energy

If we choose to feel with our Soul

Then we can open up to our true self

To feel our Soul allows us to feel

If we do not feel we cannot be

We are a shell devoid of emotion

Causing pain in the world around us

Harming those within it

These are the hollow Souls

Their Soul energy is not complete

They are energy without focus

They are the negative to the positive

They need the most help

Only then may they find solace

We must learn to love our Souls

To keep them safe

Listen to them when they talk

Enjoy each lesson that we learn

Accept our weaknesses and enhance our strengths

We can achieve this given time and patience

Patience must come from within us

We must keep an open mind

Our body needs to be pure

This gives us unity for the Soul

2
SOUL TO SOUL

Soul to Soul craved by all

A true and never ending bond

From life to life, eternal

Physical and spiritual entwine as one

That which will empower the Soul

But gentle to the touch

A deep and guiding light within

Truer than the purest honesty

Stranger than the force of life

Even when they are away

Always they remain by your side

Even when you cannot speak

They still understand your words

Your feelings are one and the same

Your hopes and dreams identical

Ideas and ambitions become as one

All that is achieved, shared as one

Both individual yet blend as one

When we look at our Soul mate

We will see our truest reflection

This may be an identical Soul

This may be our opposite Soul

Either will complete the rest of our Soul

They give a feeling of wholeness

When we are out of sync and tune

They bring us harmony and rhythm

All this happens without effort

Other Soul mates come to prepare us

Being with them helps ready your Soul

Our true Soul mate makes us feel vulnerable

The emotion is intense, from many lives

The feeling is not new, just very deep

They can see far inside to our very Self

It often unnerves us and we withdraw

Your true Soul mate will not let you go

They will reassure by their actions

The love they bring will fill your heart

Our Soul mate often differs from our ideal

The image we hold is not the reality

This brings confusion and disappointment

We choose partners that are not to be

Even though we hope they are 'the one'

They will not stay and are not supposed to

Age is unimportant be they older or younger

What matters is being Soul to Soul

Soul mates happen in many ways

Not all Soul mates stay forever

Some are here only briefly to guide us

To lead us forward to our next emotion

They help us clear out baggage

Bringing out your best qualities

Awakening a new you from inside

They always leave a lasting impression

Their effect will be for the positive

We often assume they will be like us

Sometimes they can be our mirror

Other times they are our opposite

They are our partners in our Soul

If you look at Soul mates they blend

They are together even if far apart

You will see their special connection

They will feel a deep existing bond

The connection feels like a bolt of energy

We all search for our Soul mate

Our other half

The missing half of the same coin

One cut from the same cloth

Our 'Anam Cara'

All of us wish for this

But few of us will find it

Often because we look too hard

The power of the Soul is strongest

Fate bringing Souls together

But often the road is difficult

They may challenge our patience

Often there will be time apart

Each Soul must be made ready

This often draws partners apart

This is the strongest of tests

But your Soul will reassure you

A Soul mate may soon be in your life

Other times the journey takes much longer

Whatever happens they will appear

Your Soul mate will complete your life

Even though they may cause you pain

This will pass, the energy will settle

The love will outshine all pain

Past sorrows will vanish

Peace will be restored

The timing for both has to be right

Often we are impatient, waiting

These are the hardest of times

Your Soul mate gives strength

The pain if they leave unbearable

But their return brings pure bliss

Time spent alone beneficial to you

To be with the wrong soul, negative

To blend as one with your positive

A union complete

A Soul as one

3
SOUL MOODS

Every Soul feels its life

We know this as our moods

Some we understand

Some we do not

We can all learn to listen to our Soul

But to truly hear what is being said is harder

We are our Soul

We are our moods

Both are complex

Both entwine

Each mood is a reflection of how our soul feels

This can be negative or positive

The Soul reflects where we are in life

It also understands where we should be

It holds where we have been

It also knows where we will be going

We must be our Soul to listen to ourselves

This allows us to understand our moods

We then begin to understand who we are

We can learn much from our moods

We can begin to learn why they happen

Each mood develops us as a person

This takes time and patience

Time and patience are the hardest to learn

Both will come if we are kind to self

Spiritually our Soul holds much knowledge

Becoming aware of Spirit is difficult to do

It takes the longest time

But it is our greatest need

We all strive to understand

The Soul holds our true feelings

We can pretend that all is well

But we cannot lie to our Soul

Though it seems easier at times to lie

Denial can last for a whole lifetime

This soul will be restless

Inner and outer peace may not be achieved

Often we blame others for our troubles

When the problems lie within us

Facing our self can be the hardest

But the rewards unbound

Our Soul will not lie to us

The mood in your Soul will come out

This often happens when we are not prepared

Self honesty brings inner peace

Self reflection brings outer calm

Self denial leads to a feeling of unrest

Being honest with how you feel is difficult

But difficult tasks bring the greatest rewards

The mood of your Soul is truly you

They happen to help you grow

Growth can be a challenging journey

We grow with every mood

Happy moods feel the best

Sad moods seem the longest to go

Both give the same reward to the Soul

We need to learn to embrace our moods

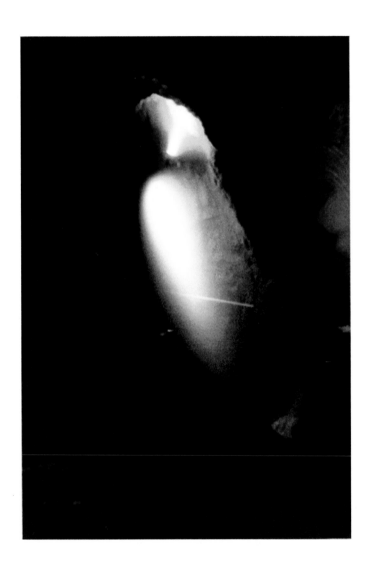

All we need to do is listen to our Soul

This brings clarity and wisdom

By doing this we can move forward

This helps ourselves and others

Both brings to us growth

To help others is an important part of life

To ignore those who need help

Is to ignore your Soul

Ignorance makes us stand still

To live is to progress

Our Soul allows us to do so

Each life makes our Soul older

Each mood reflects us

They enhance us

Often they challenge us

Many times they confuse us

Always they improve us

Ultimately they are us

To know our moods

Is to know our Soul

Is to know who we are

When we know our Soul

Then we know our moods

We learn to accept them

Because we are them

We become comfortable with who we are

We realise our moods of the past

We start to recognise our moods

We can move to our next mood with ease

All moods lead us to where we should be

Each mood holds a colour

We use colour to improve our mood

Colour can change our mood

But colour will not take the mood away

Only we can change our moods

Only we can embrace our moods

This in turn allows us to embrace ourselves

Good or bad, happy or sad

Our moods entwine and encompass us

We need our moods

We are our Soul

4

SOUL FRIENDS

We all have friends

Some are Soul mates

Our Soul mates we will keep

Others we leave behind

Some friendships are meant to go

Others are there for life

Many are old but some new

Whenever they may re-appear

You will recognise a Soul mate

These friendships stand time

Distance is irrelevant

Silence never happens

Change is encouraged

Conflict always gives it strength

Honesty is welcomed

This friendship constantly grows and adapts

It is never forced

Always it feels comfortable and safe

From life to life their role may change

Some do not stay in our lives for long

But the changes they bring are important

Some stay throughout your life

They will help you change and develop

They will understand you

There is no logic to a Soul mate

They come in many shapes and sizes

All bring many gifts of friendship

A Soul mate gives balance and harmony

This happens when yours is lost

They will make life positive

When all you can see is negative

They will banish self-denial

They will be honest with you

When you are not being honest with yourself

But they will be gentle

Theirs is a special friendship

One that no-one else can give

It is emotional

It is physical

It brings spiritual knowledge

A hug from a Soul mate heals all

A phone call at midnight is welcomed

When they hurt so do you

When they laugh so do you

There is communication without words

We feel how each other feels

We know when we need to be there

Support and understanding comes easily

At times we may be selfish

But a Soul mate allows us this

Sometimes we are self absorbed

A Soul mate will see this through

They are there for good times and bad

They share your hopes and fears

Both give without taking

Silence is never awkward but welcomed

The Souls are always talking

Even if we are not aware of this

They cheer you up

They encourage your dreams

They are never jealous of you

Always honest with love abound

Each have different qualities to bring

The give and take equals out

The recognition is instant

The friendship totally natural

It is not always easy to understand

The depth of friendship is amazing

This is because this is an old friend

A friend from a past life

A friend that your Soul recognises

An old friend to be with you

To help guide you in this life

We all have friends

We meet them through our life

Some are only there for a while

Some will always be there

Each friendship is different

But some friendships are special

A friend we have known before

These are our Soul mates

Soul mates are forever friends